Jonatas D. Sallaberry
Carlos A. P. Pereira
Eliene A. de Moraes

Valuation of Internally Generated Goodwill

Jonatas D. Sallaberry
Carlos A. P. Pereira
Eliene A. de Moraes

Valuation of Internally Generated Goodwill

A study based on the financial statements of a technology company

ScienciaScripts

Imprint

Cover image: www.ingimage.com

This book is a translation from the original published under ISBN 978-3-330-75730-1.

Publisher:
Sciencia Scripts
is a trademark of
Dodo Books Indian Ocean Ltd. and OmniScriptum S.R.L publishing group

120 High Road, East Finchley, London, N2 9ED, United Kingdom
Str. Armeneasca 28/1, office 1, Chisinau MD-2012, Republic of Moldova, Europe
Printed at: see last page
ISBN: 978-620-8-28710-8

CONTENTS

SUMMARY

Financial statements often do not reflect the market value of companies, and this difference between book value and market value is largely due to the existence of intangible assets that are not recognized in company accounting. In the accounting literature, there are several methods for valuing internally generated intangible assets, such as the Lawrence R. Dicksee method, the Hatfield method, the New York method, the current value of super-profits, replacement cost or current cost, economic value, realizable value, the excess of economic value over current value and the residual model for valuing intangible assets, each of which has advantages and disadvantages. Through exploratory research, we identified, among the methods of measuring internally generated *goodwill*, the one that effectively represents (or is closest to) the value that the market is willing to pay for the assets of a given company, considering that this difference stems from expectations of higher earnings based on surplus assets added to the entity. The research used data obtained from the 2009, 2010 and 2011 financial statements of a technology company. From the values obtained by operating the methods, it was possible to conclude that the method that comes closest to market value is the Hatfield method, with market value representing approximately six times the company's book value.

1 INTRODUCTION

The globalization of the capital market has generated the need to identify and measure the increased materiality of intangibles in the composition of entities' assets, since the accounting and financial statements often do not reflect the real value of these companies, and this difference between the accounting value and the market value is largely justified by the existence of intangible assets not recognized in accounting.

Intangible assets are responsible for the overvaluation of some companies, and these include brands, patents, advertising and publicity, *know-how*, customer confidence, the quality of the products offered, research and development, *goodwill*, intellectual capital, reputation, among others. These factors and others are added to equity as intangible assets increase in proportion to other assets due to business sophistication (MONOBE, 1986). Intangible assets add value to companies, but they cannot always be recognized and disclosed in the financial statements of the entities that generated them.

The book value of the financial statements often does not reflect the real value that could be obtained in a negotiation, generating a difference between the book value and the market value of the entity's assets, as well as its reflection in the owners' assets. According to research carried out by Machado and Famà (2011), some companies have an intangibility level of more than 8, i.e. the market is willing to pay more than 7 times what the entity is worth in accounting terms. To measure the real value of *goodwill*, assets and liabilities must have been revalued at market value, otherwise Iudicibus (2000) states that *goodwill is* a mixture of "pure goodwill" and other valuation differences.

The valuation of intangible assets is complex, especially when it comes to internally generated *goodwill*, yet there are several methods for this measurement, which are difficult to apply. Even though there are several methods, each one has advantages and disadvantages, some are complex in terms of operationalization, especially when it comes to obtaining certain variables, when these are subjective, such as the discount rate, expected profits, etc., and other variables are more relevant to certain business segments.

The aim of this paper is to identify which of the existing methods of measuring internally generated *goodwill* in the accounting literature effectively represents (or is closest to) the value that the market would be willing to pay for a given company's assets, considering that this difference stems from expectations of higher earnings based on surplus equity added to the entity.

Several studies have looked at the measurement of intangibles, such as Belém and Marques (2012), who analyzed market expectations that are not explained by the company's book value; Machado and Famà (2011) analyzed the relationship between the intangibility index and the level of Corporate Governance; Salamudin *et al.* (2010) compared the relationship between intangible assets and market value; Rodov and Leliaert (2002) contributed to the advancement of methods for measuring intellectual capital; and Wilson and Stenson (2008) identified the absence of relevant information in financial statements due to deficiencies in the measurement of intangible assets.

Other previous studies have sought to unravel the application of existing methods in the literature, including Santos *et al.* (2007) and Schmidt *et al.* (2008), who sought to present intangible measurement methods in a theoretical way. Also noteworthy is the research by Negra *et al.* (2004) which sought to operationalize the methods used by Santos and Schmidt, but using fictitious data. Rover *et al.* (2009) went one step further by using real data from a company in the electricity sector; however, they did not address which method would be closer to the companies' market value.

The importance of this research is revealed in the need for accounting science to develop methods and techniques capable of measuring internally generated intangible assets with reasonable certainty, given that theory has already proven their existence but accounting standards still restrict their recognition. This research seeks to contribute by identifying the method that presents a result closest to the real value of internally generated *goodwill*, validated by the market, in specific circumstances, considering the calculation methods that use information from financial statements.

The research also contributes to the debate on the subject of "internally generated *goodwill*" by disseminating valuation methods for this important asset.

2 INTANGIBLE ASSETS

Niyama and Silva (2011) state that intangibles may be the asset that attracts the most attention from users and accountants, and point out that intangibles are not a recent topic in accounting. The term intangible should not be confused with *goodwill* or brand, as these two make up intangible assets. The authors define the term intangible as meaning that this asset does not have a physical form, and includes, for example, brands, copyrights, customer portfolios and patents.

Intangible assets are assets that lack substance and are used to generate future economic benefits for the company (HITCHNER, 2006; HENDRIKSEN; VAN BREDA, 2011), Lev (2001) defines an intangible asset as a right to future economic benefits that does not have a financial or physical embodiment, while Martins (1972) comments that there is a real difficulty in defining it, although other authors try to show that an intangible hardly remains an asset if it is disconnected, i.e. if this intangible is separated from its context.

Santos *et al.* (2008) warn that the attempt to relate the definition of accounting to the etymology of the word would not be successful, since several assets that also lack tangibility are classified as if they were tangible, such as anticipated expenses, financial investments, among others. A better definition of these intangible assets would be to exclude items realizable until the end of the following year, based on the quote by Hendriksen and Van Breda (2011) that accountants have sought to limit the definition of intangibles by restricting it to permanent assets, i.e. non-current assets.

Flower (2002) states that it should be identified whether future economic benefits relating to intangible assets are likely and whether their cost or value can be reliably measured, as Sallaberry (2014) points out that depending on the scope of the business, the cost or value of intangible assets can account for a large part of a company's total value.

According to Salamundin *et al.* (2010), like all other assets, an intangible asset is a resource controlled by a company as a result of past events and from which future economic benefits are expected. Martins (1972, p. 30) defines an intangible asset as "the future economic result that an agent is expected to obtain.

Hoog (2008, p. 40) states that intangible assets are:

> Movable assets with no physical substance, and an economic life with a duration that is often subjective, varying in value as a result of the rights that ownership ensures, with the consequent competitive advantages and profits, and can be acquired or developed internally. Some of these Intangible Assets can be identified independently, such as a trademark, pre-operating expenses, development and research costs, *franchises and co-branding.*

The Accounting Pronouncements Committee (CPC) has defined an intangible asset as an identifiable non-monetary asset without physical substance, and emphasizes that to be considered an intangible asset, it must be identifiable, controlled by the entity and generate future economic benefits for the company (CPC 04 R1, 2010).

According to Scott (2007), intangible assets are important for many companies and, for some, they comprise the majority of the company's value. However, according to Silveira (2008), intangible assets have gained notoriety over the last three decades in the global context, although it is not a new subject, it has undergone some evolution in terms of its recognition. In Brazil, intangible assets began to have a specific group in the Balance Sheet after Law 11.638 was issued in 2007, making it possible for these intangible assets to be tested for impairment (SILVEIRA, 2008).

Law 11.638/07 states that Intangible Assets only include "rights to intangible assets intended for the maintenance of the company or exercised for this purpose, including acquired *goodwill*", with acquired *goodwill* being synonymous with *goodwill* in the Brazilian context.

As a result, copyrights, research and development expenses, trademarks, patents, concessions, *goodwill*, among others, are now included in Intangible Assets.

Iudicibus *et al.* (2009) point out that until the mid-1980s, the concern in the business world was to recognize and measure tangible assets. However, academic interest in this subject was aroused when the company Philip Morris incorporated the KRAFT food industry, which produced cheese, ice cream, etc, for 10 billion dollars, but its physical assets were accounted for at 1 billion dollars, and the additional 9 billion dollars paid for intangible assets, such as brand power, image, commercial position, etc.

A good example, in Brazil, of how intangibles add a lot of value to a company and are not recorded in its accounts, was the acquisition of Kibon by Unilever (considered one of the most significant deals to consolidate the relevance of intangible assets). Unilever paid 930 million dollars in cash in 1997 for the acquisition of Kibon. The impact was that Kibon's net equity was recorded at less than 30% of the negotiation price, thus affirming that the purchase was not of the ice cream factory, but of the Kibon brand (IUDÌCIBUS *et al.*, 2009).

Other examples can be cited, such as the acquisition of Lotus by Kibon for 3 billion dollars, while its net book value was 250 million dollars (IUDICIBUS *et al.,* 2009). According to Wernke *et al.* (2003), the values recorded and made available in financial statements, when compared to market value, distort the true and real financial position of companies. Thus, in Table 1, from the work by Booth *apud* Wernke *et al.* (2003, p. 3), we can see a comparison of the book values of some companies with their market values, and also with their estimated replacement costs.

Table 1 - Market value, booked assets and estimated replacement cost

Company	**Market value US$ billion**	**Liquid Assets US$ billion**	**Estimated replacement cost US$ billion**	**Hidden value %**
Coca-Cola	148	6	15	90
Microsoft	119	7	18	85
Intel	113	17	43	62
General Electric	169	31	77	54
Exxon	125	43	107	14

Source: Adapted from Booth *apud* Wernke *et al.* (2003).

In this sense, the net book values presented in companies' financial statements are valued differently by the market, and these higher market values represent unrecognized intangibles.

Iudicibus *et al.* (2009) point out that there are picturesque cases of famous companies that sell billions of dollars, yet produce nothing, have no factories or machines. The authors cite the example of Nike, which is the market leader in sports equipment, and most of its total assets are represented by intangibles, the company practically outsources all its products, i.e. it doesn't produce them itself.

Another interesting example is the VISA company, which generates more than 300 billion dollars a year, yet its tangible assets are negligible, being represented by furniture and fixtures, installations, etc., which could even be leased (IUDICIBUS *et al.,* 2009). The same authors point out that in a global *ranking*, Coca-Cola is generally said to be the most expensive brand in the world, followed by the following companies: Marlboro, IBM, McDonald's, Disney, Sony, Kodak, Intel, Gillete, Microsoft, etc.

Bradley (1997) states that the real values of the organizations acquired are on average four and a half times greater than the values shown in the financial statements, and that the acquisition of companies with high technical knowledge had a ratio between the acquisition value and the book value of more than ten, and these extra amounts paid in the acquisitions represent the intangible assets.

Hoss, Rojo and Grapeggia (2010) state that intangible assets are sources of sustainable advantages in competitive environments, and that these intangible assets are the intangible assets represented by the goods and rights associated with a company, and that regardless of whether they are accounted for or not, they generate value for the entity. The authors also point out that accounting is based on the transaction principle, i.e. everything that is accounted for must have gone through a transaction, whether it was bought or sold, and so it becomes difficult for the company to manage its intangible assets.

Used since the 16th century, Figure 1 shows its evolution.

Figure 1 - Timeline of intangible assets

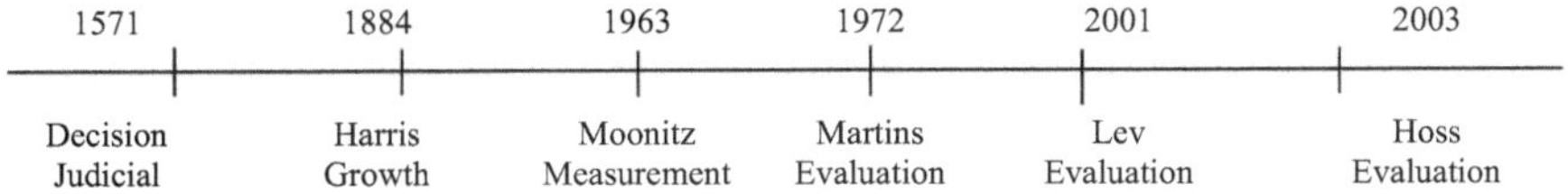

Source: Hoss *et al.*, 2010.

Over the last few decades, the relationship between market value and *book* value (*market-to-book ratio*) has expanded greatly. Lev (2001) found that the market value in some cases reaches eight times the book value of the assets, exposing the possibility of a higher valuation than the actual value of the set of assets, which was corroborated by Machado and Famà (2011). In this context, some studies have been carried out to verify the influence of intangible assets on the market value of companies (LEV; ABOODY, 1998; JOIA, 2000; CHAN; LAKONISHOK; SOUGIANNIS, 2001; CHOI; KWON; LOBO, 2000; LEV, 2001, 2003, 2004; SALAMUDIN et al, 2010; ANDRE; SOKRI; ZACCOUR, 2011).

Salamudin et al. (2010) identified the development of intangibles between 2000 and 2006, and compared the relationship between intangible assets and market value. Various studies have been carried out to explore the subject of measuring intangible assets, including Hall and Kim (1998), Rodov and Leliaert (2002), Zhang (2003), and Kent and Titman (2006), which have contributed to the advancement of methods for measuring intellectual capital, while Baglieri *et al.* (2001) have contributed to the evaluation of research development. Wilson and Stenson (2008) identified the absence of relevant information in financial statements due to deficiencies in the measurement of intangibles.

Lev (2001, 2003, 2004, 2005) is one of the main authors who has studied intangibles in the market individually or as co-author in other works (LEV; SOUGIANNIS, 1996; LEV; NISSIN; THOMAS, 2002; HAND; LEV, 2003; LEV; DAUM, 2004; LEV; RADHAKRISHMAN, 2005; LEV; RADHAKRISHMAN;

ZHANG, 2009; LEV; LI; SOUGIANNIS, 2010; LEV; RADHAKRISHMAN; TONG, 2012). They carried out various studies relating market value and intangibles, on the specific topics of recognized and unrecognized research and development, concepts, recognition and measurement. Perez and Fama (2006) also analyzed the intangibility of American companies and found that companies with a higher intensity of intangibles have superior economic performance.

The higher valuation validated by the market in relation to expenses has also been the subject of several studies such as Choi, Kwon and Lobo (2000), Chan, Lakonishok and Sougiannis (2001), Kerr and Darroch (2004), Gerpott, Thomas and Hoffman (2008) and Gilio (2010).

Choi, Kwon and Lobo (2000) analyzed the relationship between the value of recognized intangible assets and amortization expenses with the company's market value, identifying that intangible assets have a positive impact on market value, but it was not possible to establish a significant relationship between amortization expenses and stock returns. Chan, Lakonishok and Sougiannis (2001) related the *book-to-market* index to research and development expenses and found that these expenses did not explain future stock returns either.

Gerpott, Thomas and Hoffman (2008) identified that spending on marketing, training and research and development of products and technologies are the main signals for the market to expand the market value margin. Kerr and Darroch (2004) found that almost everything that organizations are able to create and which is somehow perceived by investors is part of market value, especially management capacity. The analysis of the *market-to-book* index in relation to performance, as a measure of value creation in the organization, showed a positive relationship.

According to Gilio (2010), investments in research and development have a very broad concept, such as new products and brands, as well as operational efficiency, accounted for in assets, when permitted by the standard, or recognized as general, administrative or research and development expenses in the fiscal year.

Other research has pointed to some intangible items, such as corporate reputation, which is a general organizational attribute that reflects the extent to which external stakeholders perceive the company as good rather than bad (ROBERTS; DOWLING, 2002). Green *goodwill* stems from a policy of highlighting environmental performance to the public, which affects its image and consequently its profits; according to Klassen and McLaughlin (1996) the market value of a company increases by an average of 80.5 million dollars after the announcement of an environmental award.

For identifiable intangibles, Barth et al. (1998) found results in their research which suggest that the estimates are relevant and sufficiently reliable to be reflected in share prices.

In Brazil, Machado and Famà (2011) analyzed data on the 120 largest Brazilian companies listed on BM&FBOVESPA in terms of traded value and market value between 2002 and 2007, comparing the differentiated levels of Corporate Governance with the *proxy* for intangibility - the ratio between market value and book value. The authors found that the *cluster of* companies in the Novo Mercado segment, with the highest governance practices, had a higher average intangibility, without being able to validate the hypothesis that the level of intangibility follows the governance levels.

Couto (2009) also studied the levels of Corporate Governance and identified that intangible assets have an impact on the economic performance of companies, only in part of the sample, showing that investments in intangible assets provide companies with competitive advantages.

Belém and Marques (2012) analyzed 180 companies listed on the Bovespa between 2000 and 2010 in order to identify the influence of intangible assets on return on equity. To test for differences in return on equity, the companies were organized into two groups of tangible-intensive and intangible-intensive companies. The result found that companies with higher intangible assets measured by investors through their market value were able to generate more value for their shareholders.

Fietz and Scarpin (2008) analyzed 190 companies listed in the theoretical portfolio of the IBrX Brazil index, from 2004 to 2006, in order to analyze the degree of intangibility and its relationship with accounting indices. The results of the multiple linear regression with 33 variables, one dependent (Degree of Intangibility) and 32 independent, concluded that the proposed model with accounting information enables users to determine the degree of intangibility.

Gilio (2010) studied the Brazilian companies with the largest share in the Ibovespa index in 2009 in order to analyze the explanatory power of accounting information for the *market-to-book* index, adjusted by the natural logarithm. It was found that the explanatory power of the model did not reach a considerable minimum value, showing that despite being a valid model, the selected accounting information does not have the power to explain the variation in the index.

Although the focus of the local standard related to the recognition of intangibles refers to acquired *goodwill*, patents and franchises, it is possible to broaden the meaning of intangible to the difference between the market value of the company and the book value of equity, similar to the measurement modeling used for other terms used by different scholars, such as hidden reserves (KANE; UNAL, 1990), intellectual capital (ROSS; ROSS, 1997), hidden value (EDVINSON; MALONE, 1997), reputation (ROBERTS; DOWLING, 2002) and unexplained value (LEV, 2004).

This shows the importance of the value of intangibles when evaluating a company, because generally what is sold is not the physical asset, but a set of intangible items such as the brand, image and reputation, goodwill, location, etc., because the value of tangible assets represents a derisory amount of the market value of these companies. What happens is that many of these intangible assets are difficult to measure, or have measurement methods that differ greatly in terms of the values calculated, which does not give confidence, and therefore are not recognized in company accounting.

2.1 Classification of Intangible Assets

According to Hendriksen and Van Breda (2011), intangible assets can be identifiable or non-identifiable. Assets become identifiable when they are associated with an objective description, while non-identifiable assets, as the name implies, cannot be clearly defined; the best known of these is *goodwill*. Generally speaking, Catlett and Olson (1968 *apud* SANTOS *et al.*, 2007) define *goodwill* as a benefit or advantage in the way an acquired business behaves, beyond the value it would be sold for, due to the personality of the person conducting it, the nature of its location, whether their reputation is skillful or accurate, or any other circumstance incidental to the business that tends to make it long-lasting.

Hendriksen and Van Breda (2011) cite the following intangibles as examples: product names, copyrights, franchises, *goodwill*, licenses, patents, trademarks, among others.

All the items mentioned by Hendriksen and Van Breda (2011) could, in fact, and apart from the legislation, be entered in specific intangible accounts, but it is not always possible to identify them independently of the others.

For Hitchner (2006), intangible assets also include the subsets of human capital and structural capital, with the former representing the education/training, experience and skills of a company's employees, and the latter including items such as processes and the company's organizational structure. Still according to the same author, the identification of intangible assets are the codified descriptions of specific knowledge with the characteristics of being able to be recognized and marketed.

Furthermore, the classification of intangibles can be further developed by adding measurable items, as shown in Figure 2.

Figure 2 - Classification of Intangible Assets

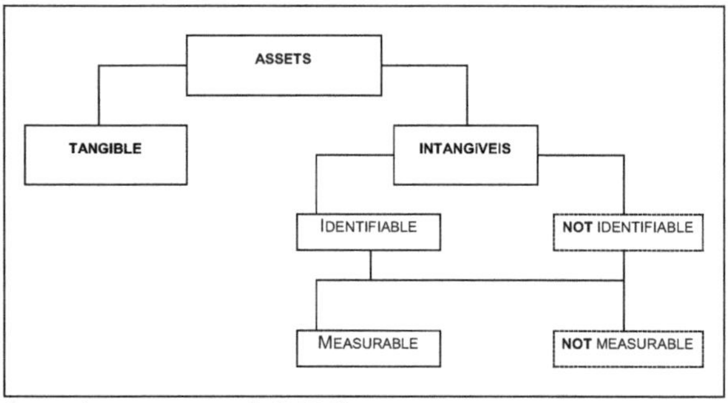

Source: Adapted from Assunçao *et al.* (2005)

Identified and measurable intangible assets (copyrights, franchises, patents); identified but not yet measurable intangible assets, such as investments in research, which added to the intangibles would not yet amount to total *goodwill.* Assuming the objective identification and measurement of each element that makes up Intellectual Capital, *goodwill* would continue to exist, according to the concept of synergistic *goodwill*[I] (ANTUNES; MARTINS, 2002; SETH; SONG; PETTIT, 2002).

Rodrigues (2011) points out that due to the complexity of measuring intangible assets,

I Synergistic *goodwill* represents the ability to generate profits from the joint use of assets that the sum of their individual capacities would not achieve.

there are various differentiations with regard to identification and classification, and emphasizes that the entity needs to know its assets, as well as the benefits generated by these assets in order to define their contribution to the company's performance.

According to Hendriksen and Van Breda (2011), intangible assets are classified according to Table 1.

Table 1 - Classification of Intangible Assets by Hendriksen and Van Breda

Intangible Assets	
Traditional Intangibles	**Deferred Expenses**
Product names	Advertising and promotion
Copyright	Advances to authors
Commitments not to run	*Software* development costs
Franchises	Costs of issuing debt securities
	Legal costs
Intangible Assets of Future Interest	*Marketing* research
Goodwill	Organizational costs
Licenses	Pre-operating expenses
Operating rights	Moving costs
Patents	Repairs
Recording matrices	Research and development spending
Secret processes	Installation costs
Trademarks	Training costs
Product brands	

Source: Adapted from Hendriksen and Van Breda, 2011.

According to Hendriksen and Van Breda (2011), there are two general classifications for intangible assets:

a) **Identifiable Intangible Assets** - assets become identifiable when they are associated with an objective description, or when this intangible asset can be given a name.

b) **Unidentifiable Intangible Assets** - occurs when it is not possible to clearly and objectively define the origin, description and control of the intangible asset.

Schmidt and Santos (2002) classify intangible assets as start-up and pre-operational costs, brands and product names, research and development, copyright, patents, franchises, *software* development, licenses, recording matrices, some long-term investments and *goodwill.*

SFAS 141, issued by the FASB in June 2001, was the first standard in the world context to define the main types of intangible assets, and also defined how to determine the separate recording of *goodwill.* According to the FASB, intangible assets can be classified into six groups: (a) intangible assets related to *marketing*; (b) intangible assets related to customers; (c) intangible assets related to the arts; (d) intangible assets related to contracts; (e) intangible assets related to technology; and (f) *goodwill.*

Gomes (2001) classifies intangible assets as follows: (a) information technology infrastructure; (b) systematization and storage of data; (c) management of trademarks and patents; (d) image management through institutional promotion of the company; (e) implementation of literacy, training and personal development programs; and (f) implementation of support and theoretical development programs for cooperative members.

Butler *et al.* (2000) cited by Hoss, Rojo and Grapeggia (2010) suggest a classification into four categories:

1) human capital, such as individual customer-solving skills, competencies and procedures;

2) customer capital, such as the strength of customer relations, superior value perceived by customers and an increase in customized solutions;

3) organizational capital, such as the organization's ability to compose knowledge and classify it into its sources such as knowledge base, business processes, shared culture, values and norms; and

4) intellectual capital, which is its ability to generate a return in assets for shareholders.

Kaplan and Norton (1997) classify intangible assets under four perspectives: (a) finances; (b) customers; (c) internal processes; and (d) learning and growth. For each perspective, the authors raise a question and try to identify objectives, indicators, targets and initiatives, as shown in Table 2.

Table 2 - Kaplan and Norton's classification of intangible assets

Grouping/Perspectives	Questioning (Vision and Strategy)
Finance	To be financially successful, how should we be seen by our shareholders?
Clients	To achieve our vision, how should we be seen by our customers?
Internal processes	In order to satisfy our shareholders and customers, in which business processes must we achieve excellence?
Learning and Growth	To achieve our vision, how do we sustain our ability to change and improve?

Source: Adapted from Kaplan and Norton, 1997.

As you can see, *there is* no consensus on the classification of intangible assets, there are numerous elements classified in different groups (RODRIGUES, 2011).

With regard to the recognition and measurement of intangible assets, the most relevant aspects will be discussed in the next section.

2.2 Recognition and Measurement of Intangible Assets

According to Hendriksen and Van Breda (2007, p. 389-390), some people argue that intangible assets should be treated differently from tangible assets, because the latter have different characteristics, such as

a) **alternative uses** - intangible assets represent the development of exclusive processes or products, or the protection of superiority in terms of *marketing*, neither of which can be transferred to alternative uses.

b) **separability** - intangible assets only have value in combination with the company's tangible assets, which makes them difficult to measure.

c) **uncertainty** - intangible assets have a high degree of uncertainty regarding the value of future benefits to be received, as possible values can vary from zero to very high amounts.

In this sense, intangible assets can be recognized when they can be identified separately from other assets, the company can control them in terms of the enjoyment of future economic benefits and their value can be measured reliably.

Recognizing an item as an intangible asset requires the entity to demonstrate that it meets the following requirements (IAS 38, N. 18-21, 2010):

a) the definition of intangible assets;

b) the recognition criteria, such as the probable enjoyment of future economic benefits generated in favor of the entity; and

c) the cost of the asset can be measured reliably

Hendriksen and Van Breda (2007, p. 388), based on paragraph 63 of SFAC 5[II] , state that an intangible asset can only be recognized "[...] *when (a) it meets the appropriate definition, (b) it is measurable (c) it is relevant, and (d) it is precise."*

These assets must also represent probable future economic benefits obtained or controlled by the entities as a result of past transactions or events, as stipulated in the definition of assets according to CPC 00 (2011).

Despite the definitions of intangible assets presented in the previous section, it should be noted that not all assets meet the definition of an intangible asset as far as recognition is concerned, because in order to be considered an intangible asset that can be recognized in a company's accounts in accordance with regulations issued by the competent bodies, it needs to be identifiable, controlled by the entity and generate future economic benefits. In addition, they must meet the concept of an intangible asset and also meet the recognition criteria.

II American standard issued by the FASB (*Financial Accounting Standards Board*), a US non-profit organization responsible for standardizing accounting procedures in the United States of America.

In the Brazilian context, according to CPC 04 (R1, 2010, item 12) to be considered identifiable, the intangible asset must meet the identification criteria (a) it is separable, i.e. it can be separated from the entity and sold, transferred, licensed, rented or exchanged, individually or together with a related contract, asset or liability, regardless of the entity's intention to use it; or (b) results from contractual or other legal rights, regardless of whether such rights are transferable or separable from the entity or from other rights and obligations.

CPC 04 (R1, 2010, item 13) states that an intangible asset is controlled by the entity when the company has "the power to obtain future economic benefits generated by the underlying resource and to restrict third party access to those benefits", and adds that generally the ability to control the future economic benefits of an intangible asset is linked to legal rights that can be exercised in court.

Niyama and Silva (2011) point out that CPC 04 restricts the scope of intangible assets in terms of recognition and measurement, and is concerned with the issue of control, as it states that the absence of legal rights makes it difficult to prove this control; however, this standard emphasizes that legal rights are not essential for the recognition or measurement of intangible assets. Thus, reliability in relation to the measurement of intangible assets is presumed, and as a result many intangible assets cannot be recognized, such as internally generated *goodwill* (NIYAMA; SILVA, 2011). According to Bergholtz and Li (2013), due to the abstract nature of internally generated goodwill, its recognition is prohibited in the entity's balance sheet.

In this sense, Sà (2008) *already* stated that since book value only includes the values recorded in the accounting books and registers, other values can be formed which are not recorded in the accounts, and he mentions "goodwill" on the value of the net worth of capital, which are immaterial values created because of their ability to produce results and also because of their ability to carry out an activity in an organized way.

Hoss, Rojo and Grapeggia (2010) point out that although intangible assets play an important role in creating value for organizations, they are not usually shown in the financial statements because of the complexity involved in measuring them.

As for the criteria for recognizing an intangible asset, CPC 04 (R1, 2010, item 21) defines that an intangible asset should only be recognized if it is probable that it will generate future economic benefits and its value can be measured reliably.

With regard to the measurement of an intangible asset, measurement methods are of fundamental importance to entities, as measuring an entity's *goodwill*, reducing distortion to its market value and/or its use is vital within a highly competitive environment (SILVA; LIMA FILHO, 2014).

CPC 04 (R1, 2010) states that when the acquisition is separate, the cost is usually the amount the company paid to acquire the intangible asset separately; and when it is an acquisition as part of a business combination, its cost should be the fair value on the acquisition date, which reflects expectations about the probability that the future economic benefits embodied in the asset will be generated in favor of the acquiring entity.

However, for accounting theory there are other assets considered intangible, which cannot be identified separately from other assets or are not reliably measurable.

In this sense, Hendriksen and Van Breda (2011) state that it is extremely difficult to measure an unidentifiable intangible asset, so much so that they end up being associated with other assets treated as residues of the asset. In cases where the intangible asset can be separated from other items such as patents and copyrights, the most informative measure would be the present value of the projected benefits, although accountants prefer to use transaction costs for their greater accuracy. For identifiable intangibles, Barth *et al.* (1998) found results in their research which suggest that the estimates are relevant and sufficiently reliable to be reflected in share prices.

Intangible assets acquired or developed through identifiable extraordinary expenses are capitalized and subsequently amortized as the benefits are enjoyed, and it is essential to indicate the useful life of the asset and the level of asset allocation (HENDRIKSEN; VAN BREDA, 2011).

In situations where the useful life of the asset is limited by legal or contractual imposition, the lifetime limit should be the point at which amortization ends, unless the duration of the economic utility exceeds the established period, which according to the authors would be difficult. The pace of amortization works in the same way as depreciation, appropriate in relation to the expected contributions to revenue or benefit flows (HENDRIKSEN; VAN BREDA, 2011).

According to Santos *et al.* (2007) intangible assets that have an indefinite useful life will not be amortized but will be tested annually for *impairment*, in accordance with paragraph 16 of SFAS 142, to check whether events or circumstances continue to justify the indefinite useful life. In Brazil, the treatment given by CPC 04 (R1, 2010) is identical.

This *impairment* test consists of "comparing the fair value of the intangible asset with the value recorded in the accounts" (SANTOS *et al.*, 2007, p. 176). When the fair value net of selling expenses of the intangible asset is greater than the book value recorded in the accounts, it is because the value is recoverable, and *there is nothing* to recognize, but if the fair value net of selling expenses is less than the book value, the difference should be recognized as an *impairment* loss.

3 GOODWILL

According to Cavalcante *et al.* (2006), research and studies on the subject of *goodwill* worldwide had their benchmark in 1968 with the publication of the research entitled "*Accounting for goodwill"* by Catlett and Olson. In Brazil, the topic was addressed in Professor Eliseu Martins' doctoral thesis, entitled "Contribuiçao à Avaliaçao do Ativo Intangivel" (Contribution to the Valuation of Intangible Assets), presented to FEA-USP in 1972.

However, Santos *et al.* (2007) point out that in England, as early as 1571, the word "*goodwill"* was used in court decisions related to land disputes. Kam (1990) cites that in 1571 the notion of *goodwill* was described in a will as an indication of the existence of the term in commercial relations, where John Stephen claims to have an interest (*goodwill*) in Quarrell's land.

Kam (1990), quoting Yang (1927), describes a case that happened in 1620, where the seller of goods agreed, as part of the purchase price, to keep new goods in his store. In this case, the buyer asked and was granted, so *goodwill* refers to the continued patronage of old customers. Kam (1990) also points out that it is not surprising that the law dealt with *goodwill* before accountants wrote about it.

The most cited court case indicating the initial notion of *goodwill* was the case of Cruttwell *v.* Lye in 1810, in which Lord Eldon made the following statement: "The *goodwill* that has been the subject of sale is nothing more than the old customers resorting to the old place", in this sense, the idea is that *goodwill* relates to the advantage of the location of the business and the habit of customers to buy there (KAM, 1990).

In 1859, in another court decision between Chuston *versus* John Douglas, the definition of *goodwill* was expanded to include all intangible advantages obtained by a company and related to its location, its name (reputation) or any other intangible that brought economic benefit to the entity, in this case, Vice-Chancellor Wood argued that when the defendant John Douglas sold the *goodwill*, he actually sold the benefits that were related to the company sold, and further explained that the definition given by Lord

Eldon was limited, in his opinion, *goodwill* meant all the advantages that were acquired together with the company in the exercise of its activities, such as the premises, as well as the name of the company, and any benefit/advantage intrinsic to such a company (KAM, 1990).

According to Kam (1990), the English courts treated *goodwill* as property or as a property right inseparable from the business, in this sense, several English and American courts from 1872 onwards came to the same conclusion, and also concluded that *goodwill* was seen as certain differential advantages for a company, advantages so valuable that they could increase its value, *goodwill* was not simply a product, but an asset.

According to Catlett and Olson (1968) cited by Santos *et al.* (2007), the first studies carried out in the accounting area on the subject of *goodwill* were still in the 19th century, dating back to 1884, with the publication of William Harris in the magazine "*The Acccountant*", entitled "*Goodwill*", and referred to the significant growth of *goodwill* in joint stock companies, and also in 1888 was published in the same magazine, with the same title, research carried out by J. H. Bourne bringing conceptual aspects regarding the subject.

Pinto (2003) cited by Negra *et al.* (2004) reports that debates on *goodwill* in English records date back to the 19th century, and cites pronouncements and publications dating back to 1891, when an article on the subject written by Francis More was read before the *Chartered Accountants Students Society of Edinburg*, Scotland, and in 1897, an article entitled *Goodwill and Its Treatment in Accounts* was published in London, written by Lawrence Robert Dicksse, in which he addressed the problems of recognizing *goodwill* in accounting, and proposed its immediate liquidation against equity in cases where it had to be accounted for.

Francis More, an accountant, advanced his studies with the argument that the valuation of *goodwill* should be based on higher profits, since *goodwill* adds value to the company, and by the 1920s, this point of view had become entrenched in the accounting literature (KAM, 1990).

In 1898, Edwin Guthrie gave a lecture, bringing aspects of the concepts proposed by Lawrence Robert Dicksee, setting out the appropriate way to adjust the company's net profit in order to obtain an adequate basis for measuring *goodwill, and* his work was also published in the magazine "*The Accountant".*

In 1909, Henry Rand Hatfield, an accounting professor at the University of California and a great scholar on the subject of intangible assets, published in his book *Modern Accounting: Its Principles and Some of Its Problems*, in New York City, a method for calculating *goodwill* (PINTO, 2003 cited by NEGRA *et al.,* 2004; SANTOS *et al.*, 2007).

In 1914, Percy Dew Leake presented a study which was also published in the journal "*The Accountant*" dealing with the subject, and this was considered a major effort in the evolution of the accounting treatment of *goodwill* in the accounting literature (SANTOS *et al.*, 2007). It is also worth mentioning the work carried out by Catlett and Olson, published in 1968 by the AICPA, entitled "*Accounting for goodwill*", which is considered a milestone in the accounting study of *goodwill* (SANTOS, *et al.,* 2007).

Santos *et al.* (2007) point out that as early as 1929, despite numerous studies on the subject, there was no single definition for *goodwill.* This is reflected in the words of Canning, who stated that many scholars had tried to define *goodwill*, discuss its nature and propose ways of measuring it, but what they had achieved was a variety of disagreements. According to Santos *et al.* (2004), these disagreements over the definition of *goodwill* continue to this day.

Rover *et al.* (2009, p. 3) point out that the definition of *goodwill "is* as imprecise as the definition of Intangible Assets", and further state that *goodwill* is the most intangible of the intangible assets, and this is due to the difficulty of separating this *goodwill* from the other intangible assets, which also makes its recognition difficult.

Thus, it is easier to define *goodwill* through its emergence, which can be, for example, through advertising, the company's location, employee training, good customer relations, technology, good relations with employees, *know-how*, the representativeness of a brand or patent, among others. Corroborating this idea, Rover *et al.* (2009) state that *goodwill* is made up of numerous factors that are not independent and cannot be sold individually, and therefore results from the synergy existing in an entity.

According to Hendriksen and Van Breda (2007, p. 390), *goodwill* "represents advantages that are not specifically identifiable", and also points out that what is lacking is a logical method that can link the costs of *goodwill* to any specific revenue in future periods, because the lack of alternative uses, the lack of separability and the uncertainty associated with its benefits prevent its recognition.

It should be noted that "*goodwill* differs from other identifiable and separable assets, which can be traded individually, because its existence is linked to the company, from which it cannot be separated or sold" (FIPECAFI, 2012).

Santos *et al.* (2007, p. 2) point out that the "definition of *goodwill,* its nature, its characteristic of not being separable from the business as a whole and its accounting treatment are among the most difficult and controversial objects of study in Accounting Theory", in this sense the authors explain that this is due to the fact that the value of *goodwill* is directly and intimately linked to other intangibles, as it is the result of the synergy between other assets.

Goodwill is the most important intangible asset for most companies, and the most complex in terms of recognition and measurement. As a result, Hendriksen and Van Breda (2009) point out that there are three main approaches to its valuation:

(1) by evaluating favorable attitudes towards the company;

(2) through the present value of the positive difference between expected future profits and the considered normal return on the total investment, not including *goodwill*; and

(3) through a general valuation account - the difference between the value of the company as a whole and the valuations of its individual tangible and intangible net assets.

In the first case, i.e. the assessment of favorable attitudes towards the company, this approach effectively suggests that the component factors of *goodwill* are as identifiable as a landmark, for example, and that *goodwill* results from the company's *good* relations with customers and employees, or good location, excellent image and reputation, good management, among other factors, all of which are favorable to the company (HENDRIKSEN; VAN BREDA, 2007).

In the second, which deals with the present value of higher profits, the approach assumes that *goodwill* is the present value of expected future profits, and that this is higher than what could be considered a normal return for the company (HENDRIKSEN; VAN BREDA, 2007).

In the third approach, i.e. *goodwill* considered as a general valuation account, from this point of view, *goodwill is* simply the value of the company that we cannot associate with specific assets, i.e. *goodwill* is treated as a closing account (HENDRIKSEN; VAN BREDA, 2007).

Iudicibus (2000) and Hendriksen and Van Breda (2007) point to three other perspectives for analyzing intangibles: (a) the excess price paid for the purchase of an enterprise over the market value of its net assets; (b) as the excess value paid by the parent company for its stake over the subsidiary's net assets; and (c) as the present value of expected future profits, discounting what would be expected to be *goodwill.*

In the first two cases, referring to objective *goodwill*, which is the amount paid to acquire a company minus the market value of the assets and liabilities, the amount is recorded in the accounts as the difference between the amount actually paid and the market value of the assets. Santos *et al.* (2007) consider that it is something extra paid over the fair value of the net equity of the acquired entity, due to a (subjective) expectation of future profits above its costs and opportunity. In order to measure the real value of *goodwill*, the assets and liabilities must have been revalued at market value, otherwise, as Iudicibus (2000, p. 2013) states "[...] Goodwill is a mixture of 'pure goodwill' and other valuation differences".

The third case, typically subjective *goodwill*, arising from the expectation of future profits generated by the company itself, is the oldest method and, according to Santos *et al.* (2007, p. 204), is "[...] through the present value of higher profits"; to do this, it is necessary to identify the normal market return for the business and reduce it by the expected future profits.

Another classification given to *goodwill* is in relation to its origin: objective or subjective. Objective *goodwill* is that acquired on the purchase of an investment of

third parties, while subjective *goodwill* is revealed when the asset is created internally within the company. In the case of accounting for expected future profits, due to the problems of complexity and subjectivity, it is also necessary to consider the application of the Accounting Principles, especially those of Opportunity and Prudence.

It should be noted that there is a difference between objective *goodwill* and subjective *goodwill*. Iudicibus *et al.* (2009) explain that objective *goodwill* is the same as acquired *goodwill*, representing the difference between the amount paid to acquire a company and the market value of the assets and liabilities acquired, and can be recognized in the accounts of the acquiring company; while subjective *goodwill* is the *goodwill* generated internally by the company and cannot be recognized due to the lack of reliability in its measurement.

Perhaps because of this difficulty in identifying and measuring them separately, some authors have come to consider *goodwill* as the value in excess of the fair price (SANTOS *et al.*, 2007). In order to better define *goodwill*, Martins (2001) and Fipecafi (2012) identified some aspects of distinction and segmentation that they consider relevant in accounting doctrine:

a) **nature of assets:** tangible and intangible;

b) **conceptions of *goodwill***: overprofits, undervaluation or failure to record assets;

c) **classification of *goodwill***: commercial, industrial, financial, political, personal, professional, intellectual capital, name or brand, etc.

d) **emergence of *goodwill***: superior management, prominent sales organization or manager, effective advertising, secret processes, intellectual capital, privileged location, favorable legislation, good relations with society and clients, etc.

Knowledge of the value of *goodwill* is important for companies because it allows them to assess the performance of managers, in the sense that the function of these managers is to maximize the value of the company for its shareholders, and the stock market itself and the corporate transactions market need this value, as stated by Fipecafi (2012).

Neiva (1999) highlights the following factors for separating *goodwill* from other intangible assets and also from tangible assets:

a) the value of *goodwill* cannot be related to the costs that may have been incurred for its creation;

b) Individual intangible factors that may contribute to the formation of *goodwill* cannot be evaluated;

c) *goodwill* belongs to the company as a whole, so it does not exist as a value separate from other assets. It is an inseparable part of the company and cannot be sold separately;

d) *goodwill* can and does fluctuate because of the many factors that influence its value;

e) the *goodwill* is not used or consumed in the production of profits; and

f) *goodwill* is an element of value that belongs to the investor or owner of the company. Only they can have an interest in determining its value by evaluating the company as a whole.

Santos *et al.* (2004, p. 5) point out that all the elements that make up *goodwill* have economic value, but due to "the lack of tangibility, the absence of cost, the difficulty of measurement, its subjectivity and the disagreement over its own role, meaning and definition", only acquired *goodwill* is recognized in accounting, i.e. that which results from the acquisition of a company.

Paton and Paton Jr. (1952) quoted by Martins (1972) classify *goodwill* as:

a) commercial *goodwill* - represents courteous sales staff, convenient deliveries, credit facilities, product quality in relation to price; consumer habit, the fruit of persistent advertising, the firm's prime location, among others.

b) industrial *goodwill* - refers to high salaries, low employee *turnover,* satisfactory internal opportunities for hierarchical access, medical service, among others.

c) financial *goodwill* - represents the ease of obtaining financing, the ability to obtain capital in the form of money, goods or services, being a renowned organization, etc.

d) political *goodwill* - refers to the company's *good* relations with the government.

It should also be noted that the term *goodwill* in Brazil has been translated as "goodwill", however, these terms have different meanings, which leads the translation to error. It is understood that the term *goodwill* is related to the *good* location of the company, while *goodwill* represents the residual value of intangible assets that cannot be identified. In this sense, goodwill, if it cannot be identified, is part of the value of *goodwill,* but the reverse is not true, as *goodwill* represents other assets besides *goodwill,* such as brands, intellectual capital, patents, good customer relations, among others.

Martins (1972, p. 55) states that using the term *goodwill* as a synonym for *goodwill* is incorrect, as *goodwill* is not a fund, as it refers to the set of monetary resources used either as a reserve or to cover extraordinary expenses, and it is not always derived from or related to the business itself.

Still on this subject, Santos *et al.* (2007, p. 2) say that the erroneous use of the term *goodwill* as a synonym for *goodwill* is due to the fact that it has been used over time to express two different meanings:

a) the term *goodwill* representing the means necessary for the operation of the entity, which is a broader concept than *goodwill,* including some tangible assets such as inventories, furniture, among others; and

b) the term goodwill representing only the intangible factors that help to obtain profits, such as strategic location, monopolistic conditions, prominent management, etc.

Iudicibus *et al.* (2009) also point out that *goodwill* is not the same as *goodwill*, as the latter also includes some tangible assets.

With regard to these recognized intangibles, Sallaberry (2014) identified that they are capable of influencing the company's market value. *Goodwill* proved to be significant at 1%, the group of intangibles at 5% and pure intangibles at 10%.

3.1 Development of accounting for *goodwill* in different countries

United States of America (USA)

According to Seetharaman, Balachandran and Saravanan (2004) *goodwill* has been debated in American literature and courts since the early 1900s, however, the first document officially standardizing the subject by the American accounting profession was issued in December 1944. Accounting Research Bulletin No. 24 issued by the Accounting Procedures Committee adopted a traditional historical approach to intangibles, including *goodwill*.

Accounting Research Bulletin No. 24 recognized two types of acquired *goodwill* and established cost as the basis for valuing intangibles; however, internally generated *goodwill* was not discussed in the standard. Acquired *goodwill* with a definite useful life should be amortized systematically, but if it has an indefinite useful life, it should be recognized at cost until there is evidence that its useful life is limited.

In August 1970, the Accounting Principles Board (APB) of the AICPA issued APB 16 on Business Combinations and APB 17 on Intangible Assets, including acquired *goodwill* (SEETHARAMAN; BALACHANDRAN; SARAVANAN, 2004). Acquired *goodwill* had to be amortized over a maximum of 40 years. And internally generated *goodwill* continued to be prohibited from being recognized in American accounting.

Canada

The Canadians followed the Americans and in December 1973 the *Canadian Institute of Chartered Accountants* (CICA) issued standard 1580 dealing with Business Combinations, applicable from March 3, 1974, which stated that acquired *goodwill* should be capitalized and amortized over a period of 40 years, and the document was also silent on the recognition of internally generated *goodwill* (SEETHARAMAN *et al.*, 2004).

New Zealand

The standard dealing with the Consolidation of Financial Statements was issued in New Zealand in 1978 (SSAP 8). In this standard, it was required that in business combinations, the acquired company be valued at fair value, and the amount paid in excess of this fair value would be considered acquired *goodwill*. SSAP 8 did not require the *goodwill* acquired to be amortized, but it had to be shown as an intangible asset on the balance sheet, to the extent that it had not been amortized.

SSAP 8 was later replaced by a new SSAP 8 which dealt specifically with Business Combinations and was issued in 1987, to be applied from January 1988, and one of the main changes was the requirement to amortize the *goodwill* acquired over the period generating future economic benefits, however, in the discussion document on the standard, it was stated that the amortization period should not be less than 10 years and more than 20 years.

Australia

In Australia, a variety of accounting practices were used to account for *goodwill* while there were no standards issued by competent bodies. It was only at the end of 1977 that the subject of *goodwill* was put on the discussion agenda of the *Australian Accounting Research Foundation* (AARF) and in December of the same year a *Discussion Paper* was commissioned. The AARF received the first draft from Ernst and Whinney in August 1978 and a revised paper in May 1980. The first exposure draft was issued 13 months later, and in May 1983, an exposure draft of the standard was put to public hearing.

Statement of Accounting Standards AAS 18, the Australian standard on accounting for *goodwill*, was issued in March 1984 to be applied from March 31, 1985. AAS 18 required acquired *goodwill* to be measured as the excess of the purchase price and the fair value of the identifiable assets acquired, recognized as an asset and amortized systematically over a maximum period of 20 years.

3.2 *Goodwill* for expected future profitability

Goodwill as an expectation of future profitability derives from the company's internal actions, and would be the oldest method, and according to Santos *et al.* (2007) is generated from the present value of higher profits. In order to measure it, it would be necessary to identify the normal market return for the business and reduce it from the expected future profits, which would imply using very subjective expectations.

In this situation, in which the company does not trade, the preferred method is to calculate the difference between the present value of future cash flows and the market value of assets and liabilities. Iudicibus (2000) reports that this value is not usually recorded due to problems of objectivity; however, it could still be estimated using the following methods:

a) Lawrence R. Dicksee's method;

b) New York method;

c) Hatfield method;

d) Present value of super profits method;

e) Replacement cost or current cost method;

f) Economic value method;

g) Realization value method;

h) Excess of economic value over current value method; and

i) Residual model for valuing intangible assets.

According to Santos *et al.* (2007) and Iudicibus (2000) internally generated *goodwill*, also known as subjective *goodwill*, can be defined as "the difference between the subjective value of the entity at a given time and the acquisition value of the assets, or also: the ability of the entity to generate profits that exceed the opportunity cost based on the initial investment valued at realizable values", however, there are problems found in the evaluation of internally generated *goodwill*, which becomes an obstacle to its recognition, such as:

a) the projection of future profit or cash flow;

b) the difficulties encountered in defining the rate to be used; and

c) problems related to the definition of the horizon.

Because of these problems, internally generated (subjective) *goodwill* is not recognized in the accounts of the company that generated it, while acquired *goodwill* can be recognized, as it represents the difference between the amount paid and the market value of the company or its net assets.

Seetharaman, Balachandran and Saravanan (2004), the valuation of internally generated *goodwill* based on a present value model or method is very subjective, as it is based on the expectation of values that may never occur, or that are incapable of confirmation.

According to Martins (1972), the biggest obstacle to recording internally generated *goodwill* is the accounting theory itself, as accountants are predominantly conservative and objective, and its recognition would be of relevance to decision-makers who have a fundamental interest in these values, especially when it comes to forecasting the future.

By considering *goodwill* as *goodwill*, or at least part of it, arising from the expectation of future profitability, it is plausible by inverse reasoning that an expectation of losses is presumed to be negative *goodwill*. This statement is defended by Santos *et al.* (2007) when they say that negative *goodwill* arises when the amount paid for the investment is less than the fair value of the net assets. According to Iudicibus (2000), this negative *goodwill* should be considered as a reserve account and its value should be transferred to the income statement within a reasonable period of time.

Along these lines, Hendriksen and Van Breda (2007) conclude that negative *goodwill* is the inverse of *goodwill*. Even so, the values of the identifiable assets would not be reduced beyond their fair value, leaving the difference between the fair value of the whole minus the amount actually paid for an intangible - negative *goodwill*. However,

Comiskey, Clarke and Mulford (2010) argue that the term goodwill would be a mistake, because a company either has goodwill (expectation of higher earnings) or it doesn't have goodwill, but it couldn't have too little goodwill, and in a context of efficient markets there wouldn't be any bargains either, showing an illusion derived from overvalued assets or unrecognized liabilities.

In the context of the expectation of future profitability, various types of intangible assets that make up intellectual capital end up being mixed with other identifiable intangible assets, such as brands and patents, and non-identifiable assets, such as *know-how*. Klein and Prusak (1994 *apud* STEWART, 1998, p. 61) define intellectual capital as "intellectual material that has been formalized, captured and leveraged in order to produce a more valuable asset". With this definition, two classes of intellectual capital can *already be* distinguished: intellectual material, which would be the separately identifiable intangible asset, and capital, which is knowledge, which according to Stewart (1998) will only be relevant in a strategic context, and its measurement will require a more complex process.

The main difference between intellectual capital, according to Schmidt and Santos (2002), is in the way they are measured: the value of subjective *goodwill* is obtained by the difference between the total economic value of the asset and its book value, i.e. the ability to generate profits that exceed costs, while intellectual capital is obtained by the difference between the market value of the entity's shares and its book value. Another difference is that intellectual capital is not recorded in the accounts and is evaluated using indicators and presented in reports or explanatory notes, while subjective *goodwill* is often recorded as if *goodwill* were a business combination.

Research expenses are also part of this expectation of future profitability, since they are incurred in order to create or improve products, resulting in future benefits for the entity, such as:

(a) activities aimed at obtaining new knowledge;

(b) search, evaluation and final selection of the applications of research results or other knowledge;

(c) searching for alternatives for materials, devices, products, processes, systems or services; and

(d) formulation, design, evaluation and final selection of possible alternatives for new or improved materials, devices, products, processes, systems or services. (CPC 04 R1, n. 55, 2010)

Intangible assets resulting from research should not be recognized, because during the research phase the entity would not be able to demonstrate the existence of intangible assets as probable generators of future economic benefits. For this reason, research costs should be recognized as an expense when incurred (CPC 04 R1, n. 53-54, 2010).

Hendriksen and Van Breda (2007) state that under the linkage concept, research and development costs should be capitalized and subsequently amortized as long as that initial investment is generating streams of economic benefits for the entity. However, expenses incurred to generate future economic benefits that do not result in the creation of an intangible asset (according to the recognition criteria) are usually described as contributions to internally generated *goodwill*, which cannot be recognized as an asset because it is not an identifiable resource (i.e. it is neither separable nor derives from contractual or other legal rights) controlled by the entity that could be reliably measured at cost (CPC 04 R1, n. 48-50, 2010).

4 METHODOLOGY

The methodology used in this work was an exploratory study, since it is carried out with the aim of providing a general and approximate view of a given subject in a methodical and organized way, using a set of intellectual and technical procedures on which scientific research depends (GIL, 1999). The exploratory study provides more information on the subject to be investigated, facilitates the delimitation of the theme, guides the setting of objectives and the delimitation of hypotheses, as well as finding new approaches to the subject, so its results can form the basis for future research (WALLIMAN, 2001).

A preliminary survey of bibliographic sources was carried out, followed by a selection of publications presenting the methods and measurement of intangible assets, especially internally generated *goodwill.* As for the research technique, it can be characterized as a case study, since it presents theories and approaches to the valuation of intangible assets for practical application in a specific company.

The typical research sequence is described as a series of stages that are expected to progress regardless of the form of the research (SMITH, 2003). In this respect, data collection was based on primary and secondary data extracted from scientific articles, technical books and the accounting and financial statements of the company analyzed. Data was collected mainly from the financial statements of the company chosen for the study, which in turn was selected arbitrarily by the authors due to the availability of accessible information.

4.1 Research Development

This research was based on the intangible asset measurement methods used by Rover *et al.* (2009), in their research entitled "Operationalization of Intangible Asset Measurement Methods in an Electricity Sector Company", where the authors present nine intangible asset measurement methods, which will be discussed below.

In this research, the company chosen to apply the measurement methods for valuing intangible assets is a multinational *software* company based in Brazil, which controls several other brands and is also considered to be the largest company in the sector based in emerging countries.

The choice of this company took into account that it is part of the *small cap* index of the São Paulo Stock Exchange, being one of the most liquid companies in this index, which is made up of companies with a lower market value and low or medium market capitalization.

As well as being one of the most liquid *small caps*, the company in the sample has one of the largest shares in the index. By using a company with a low market capitalization and lower liquidity than the companies that make up the main indices of the Sao Paulo Stock Exchange, the hope is to demonstrate whether this low level of capitalization is aligned with the value of the company's *goodwill*.

The data collected for this research was obtained from the financial statements available on the website of the São Paulo Stock Exchange for the periods 2009, 2010 and 2011, all of which ended on December 31st of those years.

4.2 Methods for Measuring Internally Generated *Goodwill*

In order to better demonstrate the measurement of intangible assets, Schmidt and Santos (2002), as well as Rover *et al.* (2009), condense and present the best-known methods of valuing internally generated *goodwill*:

a) Lawrence R. Dicksee's method

b) New York method

c) Hatfield method

d) Present Value of Surplus Profits Method

e) Replacement Cost or Current Cost Method

f) Economic Value Method

g) Realization Value Method

h) Excess of Economic Value over Current Value Method

i) Residual Valuation Model for Intangible Assets

The following section will look at the variables related to each method mentioned.

4.2.1 Choice of variables

The variables required for the operationalization of this research, as well as the values found from the data provided in the company's financial statements for 2009, 2010 and 2011, were:

Table 3 - Company data for operationalizing intangible asset valuation methods

Variable	Symbol	Value
Net Profit	LL	R$ 169,383 thousand
Management Remuneration	RA	R$ 34,220 thousand
Interest rate applicable to tangibles	I	14,23%
Tangible assets	At	R$ 58,862 thousand
Multiplicative factor for obtaining *goodwill*	F	1,301
Net Profit (average of the last two or five years)	LLm	R$ 30,212 thousand
Capitalization rate of profits	J	6%
Duration of profits or super-profits	T	15 years

Source: Prepared by the authors, 2016.

The multiplicative factor was calculated by dividing the net profit for the period analyzed by the average net profit for the previous two years, as shown in Table 2.

Table 4 - Calculation of the company's Multiplicative Factor between 2009 and 2011

	F.M.*	LL 2011	Average LL (2009-2010)	LL 2010	LL 2009
Company	1,300825	169.383	130.112	137.528	122.896
	*Multiplicative Factor				

Source: Prepared by the authors, 2016.

The interest rate for property, plant and equipment used in the calculations was obtained by calculating the midpoint between the discount rates used to calculate the cash flow of the cash-generating units, which ranged from 7.85% to 20.6%, according to the information in note 12.2 - Analysis of the recoverable value of assets.

The capitalization rate of profits was obtained according to the Long-Term Interest Rate (TJLP), a probable scenario, in BNDES financing operations, as informed by the company in note 22, letter "c".

4.2.2 Traditional methods

We will present each of the nine methods, as well as their formulas and variables.

4.2.2.1 Lawrence R. Dicksee method

Schmidt *et al.* (2008) reveal that this is considered by scholars to be the oldest method of valuing intangible assets, dating back to 1897 and based on the application of a multiplying factor to current net income.

According to Negra *et al.* (2004), one of the disadvantages of this method is that, as it is based on the net profit of the period prior to its calculation, it leads to distortions if companies show variability in their long-term results.

The Lawrence R. Dicksee method uses the following formula to calculate intangible assets:

$$G = [(LL - RA) - (i \, x \, At)] \, x \, F \qquad (1)$$

Where:

G = value of *goodwill*

LL = net profit

RA = management remuneration

i = interest rate applicable to tangible fixed assets

At = tangible assets

F = multiplicative factor for obtaining *goodwill*

Calculation by the Lawrence R. Dicksee Method

$$G = [(LL - RA) - (i \; x \; At)] \; x \; F$$

G = [(169.383 -34.220) – (0,1423 x 58.862)] x 1,301

G = 164,931 thousand

Taking into account the data presented in the company's financial statements for 2009, 2010 and 2011, according to the Lawrence R. Dicksee method, the value of its *goodwill* is R$ 164,931 (one hundred and sixty-four million, nine hundred and thirty-one thousand reais).

The main limitations of this method according to Schmidt *et al.* (2008) are: (a) using net profit as the basis for measurement instead of cash flow; (b) not defining how the multiplied factor for obtaining *goodwill* should be calculated; (c) not defining the interest rate applicable to property, plant and equipment; and (d) using the concept of retained earnings as a fixed factor, which only applies to companies with stable growth.

4.2.2.2 New York method

The calculation formula of the New York Method is practically the same as that used by the Lawrence R. Dicksee Method, differing only by the change in net profit which is replaced by the average of the last two or five years, as follows:

$$G = [(LLm - RA) - (\; i \; x \; At)] x \; F \qquad (2)$$

Where:

G = value of *goodwill*

LLm = net profit (average of the last two or five years)

RA = management remuneration

i = interest rate applicable to tangible fixed assets

At = tangible assets

F = multiplicative factor for obtaining *goodwill*

Calculation by the New York Method

$$G = [(LLm - RA) - (i \times At)] \times F$$

G = [(130.212 – 34.220) – (0,1423 x 58.862)] x 1,301

G = 113,977 thousand

Taking into account the data presented in the company's financial statements for 2009, 2010 and 2011, calculating the value of *goodwill* using the New York method, we arrive at a value of R$ 113,977 (one hundred and thirteen million, nine hundred and seventy-seven thousand reais).

According to Schmidt *et al.* (2008) this method dates back to 1898, and as it is identical to the Lawrence R. Dicksee method, its limitations are also similar to those of that method.

4.2.2.3 Hatfield method

Negra *et al.* (2004) states that the Hatfield method introduces the residual view of *goodwill*. This method dates back to 1904, and is the first valuation method to use the net present value methodology to obtain the value of the company as a whole, and after deducting the value of tangible assets, the value of intangible assets (SCHMIDT *et al.*, 2008). The formula for applying the Hatfield Method is:

$$\mathrm{G} = \frac{LL-RA}{j} - \mathrm{At} \qquad (3)$$

Where:

G = value of *goodwill*

j = profit capitalization rate

RA = directors' remuneration

LL = net profit

At = tangible assets

Hatfield Method Calculation

$$G = \frac{LL - RA}{j} - At$$

$$G = \frac{169.383 - 34.220}{0,06} - 58.862$$

$$\mathbf{G = 2.193.855}\ \boldsymbol{mil}$$

Taking into account the data presented in the company's financial statements for 2009, 2010 and 2011, the Hatfield Method reveals a *goodwill* value of R$ 2,193,855 (two billion, one hundred and ninety-three million, eight hundred and fifty-five thousand reais).

According to Schmidt *et al.* (2008) the limitations of the Hatfield Method are: (a) it uses net profit as the basis of value and not cash flow; (b) it does not define how the rate of capitalization of profits should be calculated; (c) it does not define the valuation criteria for tangible assets; (d) it does not define how the interest rate applicable to tangible fixed assets should be calculated; and (e) it uses the concept of retained earnings as a fixed factor, which only applies to companies with stable growth.

4.2.2.4 Present Value of Surplus Profits Method

Schlüter (2010) states that the earliest advocate of this method was Percy Dew Leake, who considered the gradual decrease in excess profits. According to Schmidt and Santos (2002), the Present Value of Excess Profits Method is one of the most widely used methods for valuing intangible assets and is the method that comes closest to economic value, and its calculation does not include any intangible assets. The mathematical formula for applying the Present Value of Earnings Method is:

$$G = \sum_{t=1}^{K} \frac{LL_t - RA - i\ x\ At}{(1+r)^t} \qquad (4)$$

Where:

G = value of *goodwill*

LLt = net profit at time t, which would be decreasing r = discount rate attributed to super-profits t = duration of super-profits

RA = directors' remuneration i = interest rate on tangible fixed assets

At = tangible assets

Calculation by the Present Value of Surplus Profits Method

$$G = \sum_{t=1}^{K} \frac{LL_t - RA - i \; x \; At}{(1+r)^t}$$

G = [(169.383 – 34.220)/8.373]/((1+0,06)^15)

G = 52.905 mil

Taking into account the data presented in the company's financial statements for 2009, 2010 and 2011, applying the Present Value of Surplus Profits Method, the company has *goodwill* in the amount of R$ 52,905 (fifty-two million, nine hundred and five thousand reais).

Negra *et al.* (2004) point out that this method calculates the present value of super-profits and does not include the value of intangible assets. Schmidt *et al.* (2008) points out that this method has the same limitations as the Lawrence R. Dicksee, New York and Hatfield methods.

4.2.2.5 Replacement Cost or Current Cost Method

Schmidt and Santos (2002) state that this is one of the most widely used methods for approximating the economic value of intangible assets and is obtained using the following mathematical formula:

$$G = \sum_{t=1}^{n} \frac{LL_t}{(1+R)^t} - PLcc \qquad (5)$$

Where:

G = value of *goodwill*

LL_t = net profit at time t

PL_{cc} = equity at current costs

R = opportunity cost of investment with equal risk T = duration of profit.

Negra *et al.* (2004) mention that this is considered a mixed process, which consists of measuring total assets at their economic value and the respective values at current cost.

Schmidt *et al.* (2008) point out that the model has the following limitations in its application: (a) the use of net profit as the basis for measurement instead of cash flow; (b) it does not define how the opportunity cost of equal-risk investment should be calculated; and (c) it considers that profit grows at a fixed rate, which is not considered by all companies, only those with stable growth.

Rover *et al.* (2009) state that this is a method that is difficult to operationalize, as the variables involved are not easily identified, so it is noteworthy that it was not possible to calculate the value of *goodwill* for the company using the Replacement Cost or Current Cost Method because the accounting and financial statements together with the explanatory notes and the management report did not disclose data for the calculation of all the variables contained in the mathematical formula.

4.2.2.6 Economic Value Method

According to Schlüter (2010) this method is characterized as the ideal method for valuing intangible assets, however it is difficult to implement, the author also mentions that the method was described by Professor Eliseu Martins in his doctoral thesis in 1972. The Economic Value Method is obtained using the following mathematical formula:

$$Ai = \frac{Vt}{(1+j)^t} + \sum_{t-1}^{n} \frac{R_t}{(1+j)^t} \qquad (6)$$

Where:

Ai = economic value of the asset

Vt = residual value of the asset

j = opportunity cost of an equal-risk venture

Rt = economic result produced by the asset

n = time horizon

Schmidt *et al.* (2008) highlight the following shortcomings of the method: (a) the use of the economic result as the basis for measurement instead of cash flow; (b) no

(c) considers that profit grows at a fixed rate of interest, but disregards that this type of calculation is only reasonable for companies with constant growth; (d) does not include tangible and intangible assets that do not currently produce revenue; and (e) is only useful for evaluating individual tangible assets, but not intangible assets, as these have no appreciable residual value.

It should be noted that it was not possible to calculate the value of *goodwill* for the company using the Economic Value Method, as the accounting and financial statements together with the explanatory notes and management report did not disclose data for calculating the model's component variables.

4.2.2.7 Realization Value Method

Negra *et al.* (2004) state that this model was developed by Professor Sérgio de Iudicibus, and treats internally generated *goodwill* at its net realizable value, brought to present value by a desired rate of return, using the following mathematical formula:

$$G = \left(\frac{L_i - (PL_0\ x\ R)}{1+j}\right) + \frac{(\ldots + Ln - PL_{n-1}\ x\ R)}{(1+j)^n} \qquad (7)$$

Where:

G = value of *goodwill*

PL = net equity in 2007

R = rate of return on a zero-risk investment

L_i = projected profit for period i - 2008 j = desired rate of return

Rover *et al.* (2009) state that the advantage of using this method is that it calculates *goodwill* throughout the company's existence, and further state that its main disadvantage is the projection of profit and the way in which the estimate is obtained over a long-term period.

It should be noted that it was not possible to calculate the value of *goodwill* for the company because the financial statements, together with the explanatory notes and the management report, did not provide sufficient data to calculate all the variables used in the model.

4.2.2.8 Economic Excess over Current Value Method

According to Rover *et al.* (2009), the advantage of applying this method lies in the use of assets at current costs, but they point to the complexity of the method as its main disadvantage, including the understanding of each variable, and that misinterpretation can cause distortions in the value calculated. The mathematical model for calculating the Economic Excess over Current Value Method is:

$$EVE = \left\{[(Vt\,/\,(1+R)^{t})] + \sum_{i=1}^{n}[(Rt\,/\,(1+R)^{t}) - Acc]\right\} \qquad (8)$$

Where:

EVE = excess of economic value over current value

Vt = residual value of the asset

R = opportunity cost of an equally risky venture n = time horizon

Rt = economic result produced by the asset

Acc = asset valued at current cost

It should be noted that it was not possible to calculate the value of *goodwill* for the company because the accounting and financial statements, together with the explanatory notes and the management report, did not disclose the data needed to calculate the variables in the model.

4.2.2.9 Residual Valuation Model for Intangible Assets

In his doctoral thesis, Santos proposed a new methodology for calculating *goodwill*, called the Residual Model for Valuing Intangible Assets. According to Santos *et al.*

(2007), the justification for using the residual model for valuing intangible assets is that this method differs from the main models proposed for valuing intangible assets, which use net profit as the basis for valuation and the proposed model uses the future cash flow to be produced by the assets. The mathematical formula proposed for this model is:

$$AI = \sum_{t=1}^{t=n} \left(\frac{FCFF_t}{(1 + WACC)^t} \right) + \frac{FCFF_{n+1} \,/\, (WACC - g_n)}{(1 + WACC)^n} + AIcI + PC - ATcc \quad (9)$$

Where:

AI = value of intangible assets

AIcI = value of intangible assets that meet the legal criterion and are not producing revenue, calculated using the Black-Scholes model

FCFFt = company cash flow in year t

$FCFF_n$ = company cash flow in year n (stable period)

WACC = weighted average cost of capital (Kpl using CAPM)

$WACC^n$ = weighted average cost of capital at steady state

CP = current liabilities at market value

g_n = growth rate in the period of stability

It should be noted that it was not possible to calculate the value of *goodwill* for the company because the financial statements, together with the explanatory notes and the management report, did not provide sufficient data to calculate all the variables.

4.3 Valuation at Market Value

The market value of the company as of December 2011 is determined by multiplying the weighted average number of the company's ordinary shares as of December 31, 2011 by the closing price of the share on the last trading session of 2011 in which the share was traded.

The weighted average of the company's ordinary shares can be found in note 26 and represents a total of 158,073 thousand ordinary shares. The closing price of the share in the last trading session of 2011 in which the share was traded, which took place on December 29, 2011, was R$ 33.26 per common share, as shown on the website of the São Paulo Stock Exchange (Bovespa).

As a result, the company's market value on 31/12/2011 was approximately R$5,257,508 thousand.

5 ANALYSIS OF RESULTS

Table 5 was drawn up to present the values obtained through the operationalization of each method for valuing the company's intangible assets.

Table 5 - Results of the operationalization of intangible asset valuation methods

Valuation method for intangible assets	Value in millions of R$
Lawrence R. Dicksee	164.931
New York	113.977
Hatfield	2.193.855
Current Value of Super Profits	52.905

Source: Prepared by the authors, 2016.

The methods Replacement Cost or Current Cost, Economic Value, Realization Value, Excess of Economic Value over Current Value and the Residual Model were abandoned due to the lack of data in the financial statements, explanatory notes and management report that would enable all the variables to be obtained. It should be noted that in the other models the variables were identified explicitly or from data disclosed in the statements, which makes the models applicable to audiences who do not have access to the companies' internal data.

It can be seen that of the nine methods mentioned, the simplest to apply are the Lawrence R. Dicksee, New York and Hatfield methods. The other methods are more complex and their variables are difficult to obtain because they are not available to the public.

It should be noted that the values calculated using the Lawrence R. Dicksee, New York, Hatfield and Current Value of Surplus Profits methods differ, and comparing them to the company's market value, which was R$ 5,257,508 (five billion, two hundred and fifty-seven million and five hundred and eight thousand reais) minus the accounting net equity of R$ 749.867 (seven hundred and forty-nine million, eight hundred and sixty-seven thousand reais) results in a market value of R$ 4,504,641 (four billion, five hundred and four million, six hundred and forty-one thousand reais) above the company's book value.

With these results, it can be said that the method that comes closest to the value of *goodwill* assessed by the market is the Hatfield Method, which showed a value of R$2,193,855 (two billion, one hundred and ninety-three million, eight hundred and fifty-five thousand reais). It should be noted that although the Hatfield method is the closest to the difference between the company's market value and book value, it is only able to explain 48.7% of this difference.

6 FINAL CONSIDERATIONS

Intangible assets represent, at the current moment in the evolution of accounting knowledge, one of the strongest and richest subjects in terms of field for research; as we approach intangibles and try to identify, define and measure them, we realize how synergistic and intricate the concepts and their quantitative operationalization are.

Based on the valuation of the company under study in this research, it was possible to identify the method of valuing internally generated *goodwill* that is closest to the market's pricing of the company, revealing itself to be well above the entity's book value, considering an expectation of profitability on the part of the company's operations and its assets that cannot be observed in the accounting and financial statements. Thus, it was possible to conclude that the internally generated *goodwill*, valued by the market, represents approximately 6 (six) times the company's book value, in the specific situation.

The result indicated by the Hatfield Method was the closest to the value of *goodwill* assessed by the market based on the data of the company in the sample, although it was only able to explain 48.7% of this difference, corroborating the results found by Pereira, Moraes and Sallaberry (2013).

The aim of this research, which did not intend to exhaust the subject, was to clarify the basic concepts of the most relevant aspects in the treatment of intangibles, internally generated *goodwill*, as well as evidence on measurement methods; in addition, there was an awareness of the difficulty of dealing with the subject and the intention to seek further research on the subject, especially in the field of intangible measurement, by means of a practical case.

Further research suggests the possibility of applying the Hatfield Method to other companies in the same business segment to validate the evidence found, or even applying the methods to a larger sample, segregated by market segment.

REFERENCES

ANDRE, F.J.; SOKRI, A.; ZACCOUR, G. Public Disclosure Programs vs. traditional approaches for environmental regulation: Green goodwill and the policies of the firm. **European Journal of Operational Research**, Amsterdam, n. 212, p. 199-212, 2011.

ANTUNES, M. T. P; MARTINS, E. Intellectual Capital: truths and myths. **Revista Contabilidade e Finanças -** USP, Sao Paulo, n. 29, p. 41-54, mai/ago, 2002.

ASSUNÇÂO, A. B. A.; SILVA, G. S.; SILVA, N. L. R. M.; LIMA, C. S. F. Intangible Assets: *Goodwill* or Intellectual Capital. In: CONGRESSO USP DE INICIAÇÂO CIENTiFICA EM CONTABILIDADE, 2., 2005, Sao Paulo. **Proceedings...** Sao Paulo: USP, 2005.

BAGLIERI, E. et al. Evaluating Intangible Assets: the Measurement of R&D Performance. March, 2001. **Research Division Working Paper N. 01/49**. Available at: < http://papers.ssrn.com/sol3/papers.cfm?abstract_id=278260>. Accessed on: May 18, 2013.

BARTH, M. E. *et al.* Brand values and capital market valuation. **Review of Accounting Studies.**Berkeley, vol. 3, p. 41-68, 1998.

BELEM, V. C.; MARQUES, M. M. The influence of intangible assets on the return on equity of Brazilian companies. In: CONGRESSO USP DE CONTROLADORIA E CONTABILIDADE, 12., 2012, Sao Paulo. **Proceedings...** Sao Paulo: USP, 2012.

BERGHOLTZ, J.; LI, A. Goodwill hunting? A study on the proportion of purchase price allocated to *goodwill* under IFRS. **Master Thesis in Accounting and Financial Management**. Stockholm School of Economics. Spring 2013. Available at < http://arc.hhs.se/download.aspx?MediumId=1931> Accessed on: Aug. 4, 2013.

BOVESPA. **Sao Paulo Stock Exchange**. Available at: <http://www.bmfbovespa.com.br>. Accessed on: July 1, 2012 and July 5, 2012.

BRADLEY, K. Intellectual Capital and the New Wealth of Nations. **Business Strategy Review.** Vol. 8, Issue 1, March, 1997, pages 53-62. Available at: <http://onlinelibrary.wiley.com/doi/10.1111/1467-8616.00007/full>. Accessed on:

May 23, 2016.

CAVALCANTE, P. R. N.; CALDAS NETO, C.; ANDRADE, G. M. Intellectual Capital and Goodwill: Intangible Assets that are Difficult to Measure. **Pensar Contàbil,** vol. 8, n° 33, 2006. Available at: <http://www.atena.org.br/revista/ojs-2.2.3-06/index.php/pensarcontabil/article/view/21>. Accessed on: May 23, 2016.

CHAN, L. K. C.; LAKONISHOK, J.; SOUGIANNIS, T. The stock market valuation of research and development expenditures. **The Journal of Finance**, [s. l.], v. 56, n. 6, p. 2431-2456, 2001.

CHOI, W. W.; KWON, S. S.; LOBO, G. J. Market Valuation of Intangible Assets. **Journal Business Research**, [s. l.], n. 49, p. 35-45, 2000.

COMISKEY E.; CLARKE, J. E.; MULFORD, C. **Is Negative Goodwill Valued by Investors?** Accounting Horizons. Sarasota, v. 24, n. 3, p. 333-353, 2010.

COMMITTEE OF ACCOUNTING PRONOUNCEMENTS (CPC). **Basic Conceptual Pronouncement (R1) - Conceptual Framework for the Preparation and Disclosure of Accounting and Financial Reports.** Available at:

<http://static.cpc.mediagroup.com.br/Documentos/147_CPC00_R1.pdf>. Accessed on: 06 May 2016.

. **Technical Pronouncement 04 (R1) - Intangible Assets.** Available at: <http://static.cpc.mediagroup.com.br/Documentos/187_CPC_04_R1_rev%2008.pdf>. Accessed on: 06 May 2016.

COUTO, P. B. **Intangible Assets and the Economic Performance of New Market Companies**. 2009. 134 f. Dissertation (Master's Degree in Accounting) - Center for Postgraduate Studies and Research in Accounting and Controllership, Federal University of Minas Gerais, Belo Horizonte, 2009.

EDVINSON, L.; MALONE, M.S. **Intellectual Capital: Realizing your Company's True Value by Finding its Hidden Brainpower**. New York: Harper Business, 1997.

FIETZ, E. E. Z.; SCARPIN, J. E. Study of the Degree of Intangibility through

Accounting Statements. In: CONGRESSO USP DE CONTROLADORIA E CONTABILIDADE, 8., 2008, Sao Paulo. **Proceedings...** Sao Paulo: USP, 2008.

FASB. **Financial Accounting Standards Board.** Available at: <http://www.fasb.org/fome>. Accessed on: March 20, 2012.

FIPECAFI. **Valuation of companies:** from accounting to economic measurement/FIPECAFI; Eliseu Martins (Organizer). Sao Paulo: Atlas, 2012.

FLOWER, J. **Global Financial Reporting.** New York: Palgrave, 2002.

GERPOTT T. J.; THOMAS S. E.; HOFFMAN A. P. Intangible asset disclosure in the telecommunications industry. **Journal of Intellectual Capital**. [s. l.], v. 9, n. 1, p. 37, 2008.

GILIO, L. Analysis of the Explanatory Capacity of Accounting Information for the Market-To-Book Index of Companies Listed on IBOVESPA. In CONGRESSO USP DE CONTROLADORIA E CONTABILIDADE, 10., 2010, Sao Paulo. **Proceedings...** Sao Paulo: USP, 2010.

GOMES, V. **The management of intangible assets in an agro-industrial cooperative based on the model proposed by K. e. Sveiby.** 2001. Dissertation (Master's Degree) - Federal University of Santa Catarina, Florianopólis.

HALL, B; KIM, D. **Valuing Intangible Assets**: the Stock Market Value of R&D Revisited, [s. l.], UC Berkeley - Harvard University - NBER, 1998.

HAND, J.; LEV, B. **Intangible Assets**: values, measures, and risks. London: Oxford University Press, 2003.

HENDRIKSEN, E. S.; VAN BREDA, M. F. **Teoria da Contabilidade.** Sao Paulo: Atlas, 2011.

. **Theory of Accounting.** 5ª ed. Sao Paulo: Atlas, 2007.

HITCHNER, J. R. **Financial Valuation:** applications and models. 2nd ed. Hoboken: Wiley, 2006.

HOOG, W. A. Z. **Fundo de Comércio *Goodwill* em:** apuraçao de haveres, balanço patrimonial, dano emergente, lucro cessante, locação não residential. Curitiba: Juruà Editora, 2008.

HOSS, O.; ROJO, C. A.; GRAPEGGIA, M. **Management of Intangible Assets:** from measurement to competitiveness by scenarios. Sao Paulo: Atlas, 2010.

IUDCIBUS, S. **Teoria da Contabilidade.** 7th ed. Sao Paulo: Atlas, 2000.

IUDCIBUS, S.; MARION, J. C.; FARIA, A. C. **Introduçao à Teoria da Contabilidade.** 5th ed. Sao Paulo: Atlas, 2009.

JOIA, L. A. Measuring Intangible Corporate Assets: Linking Business Strategy with Intellectual Capital. **Journal of Intellectual Capital**, Bradford, v. 1, n.1, p. 68-84, 2000.

KAM, V. **Accounting theory**. 2. ed. California: John Wiley & Sons, 1990.

KANE, E.J.; UNAL, H. Modeling structural and temporal variation in the market's valuation of banking firms. **The Journal of Finance**, [s. l.], v. 14, n. 1, 1990.

KENT, D.; TITMAN, S. Market Reactions to Tangible and Intangible Information.

Journal of Finance, [s. l.], n. 61, v. 1, aug. 2006.

KERR G.; DARROCH J. Performance in the contemporary conglomerate. **Academy of Strategic Management Journal**. [s. l.], v. 3, p. 21-32, jan. 2004.

KLASSEN, R.D.; MCLAUGHLIN, C.P. The impact of environmental management on firm performance. **Management Science**, [s. l.], n. 42, n. 8, p. 1199-1214, 1996.

KAPLAN, R. S.; NORTON, D. P. **The strategy in action balanced scorecard.** 5ª ed. Sao Paulo: Campus, 1997.

LEV, B. **Intangibles:** management, measurement, and reporting. Washington, D.C., Brookings Institution Press, 2001.

LEV, B.; SOUGIANNIS, T. The capitalization, amortization, and value-relevance of R&D. **Journal of Accounting and Economics**, [s. l.], v. 21, p. 107-138, 1996.

LEV, B.; ABOODY, D. The Value Relevance of Intangibles: the case of software capitalization. **Journal of Accounting Research**, Chicago, v. 36, supplement, p.1-43,

1998.

LEV, B.; NISSIM, D.; THOMAS, J. On the Informational Usefulness of R&D Capitalization and Amortization. **Working Paper**. Columbia Univ., School of Business. Columbia University, New York, 2002.

LEV, B. Remarks on the Measurement, Valuation, and Reporting of Intangible Assets. **FRBNY Economic Policy Review**, New York, v. 9, n. 3, p. 17-22, set. 2003.

. Sharpening the intangibles edge. **Harvard Business Review**, Cambridge, v. 82, n. 6, p. 109-16, 2004.

LEV, B.; DAUM, J.H. The dominance of intangible assets: consequences for enterprise management and corporate reporting, **Measuring Business Excellent**, [s. l.], v. 8, n. 1, p. 6-17, 2004.

LEV, B. Intangible Assets: concepts and measurements. **Encyclopedia of Social Measurement,** New York, v. 2, p. 299-305, 2005.

LEV, B.; RADHAKRISHNAN, S. The Valuation of Organization Capital, in Measuring Capital in the New Economy. **National Bureau of Economics Research**, Chicago, p. 73-99, 2005.

LEV, B., RADHAKRISHNAN, S.; ZHANG, W. Organization Capital. **Abacus**, [s. l.], v. 45, n. 3, p. 275-298, 2009.

LEV, B.; LI, S. Y.; SOUGIANNIS, T. The usefulness of accounting estimates for predicting cash flows and earnings. **Review of Accounting Studies**, [s. l.], v. 15, n. 4. p. 779-807, 2010.

LEV, B.; RADHAKRISHNAN, S.; TONG, J. Y. Risk Management for Tangible and Intangible Investments: the Relationship between R&D and Capital Expenditures and Risk Components. **Working Paper**, New York, 2012.

MACHADO, J. H.; FAMA, R. Intangible Assets and Corporate Governance in the Brazilian Capital Market. In: CONGRESSO USP DE CONTROLADORIA E CONTABILIDADE, 11. 2011, Sao Paulo. **Proceedings...** Sao Paulo: USP, 2011.

MARTINS, E. **Contribution to the valuation of intangible assets.** 1972. 107 Thesis (Doctorate in Accounting) - University of Sao Paulo - USP, Sao Paulo, 1972.

. **Company Valuation:** from accounting to economic measurement. Sao Paulo: Atlas, 2001.

MONOBE, M. **Contribution to the Measurement and Accounting of Goodwill Acquired.** Sao Paulo, 1986. Thesis (Doctorate). Faculty of Economics, Administration and Accounting, University of Sao Paulo.

NEGRA, C. A. S.; NEGRA, E. M. S., PIRES, M. A. A.; RESENDE FILHO, N. S.; LAGE, W. M. L.; COUTINHO, W. R. **Discussion, Measurement and Valuation of *Goodwill*: From Theoretical Issues to Business Practice.** Available at: < http://www.peritoscontabeis.com.br/trabalhos/goodwill_-cladea_e_17cbc.pdf>. Accessed on: July 4, 2012.

NEIVA, R. A. **Valor de mercado da empresa.** 3ª ed. Sao Paulo: Atlas, 1999.

NIYAMA, J. K.; SILVA, C. A. T. **Teoria da Contabilidade.** 2a ed. Sao Paulo: Atlas, 2011.

PEREIRA, C. A. P.; MORAES, E. A.; SALLABERRY, J. D. Valuation of internally generated goodwill through market value: a study based on the financial statements of a technology company. **Revista de Gestâo, Finanças e Contabilidade,** v. 3, n. 1, p. 53-70, 2013.

PEREZ, M. M.; FAMA, R. Intangible Assets and Corporate Performance. **Revista Contabilidade e Finanças**, Sao Paulo, n. 40, p. 7-24, 2006.

ROBERTS, P. W.; DOWLING, G. R. Corporate Reputation and Sustained Superior Financial Performance. **Strategic Management Journal**, [s. l.], n. 23, p. 1077 - 1093, 2002.

RODOV, I.; LELIAERT, P. FiMIAM: financial method of intangible assets measurement. **Journal of Intellectual Capital,** United Kingdom, vol. 3, n. 3, p. 323-336, 2002.

RODRIGUES, L. C. S. **Intangible Assets: An explanation of the main valuation techniques accepted by the accounting community.** A preparation for use in favor of competitive advantage. Monograph, 2011. Porto Alegre, Rio Grande do Sul. School of Accounting Sciences of Rio Grande do Sul.

ROSS, G.; ROSS, J. Measuring your company's intellectual performance. **Long Range Planning**, [s. l.], v. 30, n. 3, 1997.

ROVER, S.; SILVEIRA, F. N. S.; ENSSLIN, S. R.; REINA, D. Operationalization of Intangible Asset Measurement Methods in an Electricity Sector Company. In: CONGRESSO USP DE CONTROLADORIA E CONTABILIDADE, 9, 2009, Sao Paulo. **Proceedings...**Sao Paulo: USP, 2009.

SA, A. L. **Teoria da Contabilidade.** 4ª ed.. 2ª reimp. Sao Paulo: Atlas, 2008.

SALAMUDIN, N.; BAKAR, R.; IBRAHIM, M. K.; HASSAN, F. H. Intangible assets valuation in the Malaysian capital market. **Journal of Intellectual Capital,** United Kingdom, v. 11, n. 3, p. 391-405, 2010.

SALLABERRY, J. D. **Relationship between Intangible Assets and the Market Value of Brazilian Companies.** Master's thesis. 99f University of Brasilia. School of Economics, Business Administration, Accounting and Actuarial Sciences. Multi-institutional and Interregional Postgraduate Program in Accounting Sciences, Brasilia, 2014.

SANTOS, J. L.; SCHMIDT, P.; FERNANDES, L. A.; MACHADO, N. P. **Accounting theory:** introductory, intermediate and advanced. Sao Paulo: Atlas, 2007.

SCHLÜTER, M. S. **Study of the Valuation of Intangible Assets**. 2010. 56 f.

Dissertation (Master's Degree in Economics) - Postgraduate Program in Economics, Federal University of Rio Grande do Sul, Porto Alegre, 2010. Available at: <http://www.lume.ufrgs.br/handle/10183/25781>. Accessed on: July 1, 2012.

SCHMIDT, P.; SANTOS, J. L. **Valuation of intangible assets.** Sao Paulo: Atlas, 2002.

.; SANTOS, J. L.; FERNANDES, L. A.; GOMES, J. M. M.; MACHADO, N. P.. Residual Model for Measuring Intangible Assets. **Revista de Educaçâo e Pesquisa em Contabilidade** - REPeC, v. 2, n. 2, p. 18-37, 2008.

SCOTT, W. R. **Financial accounting theory.** Toronto: Prentice Hall, 2007.

SEETHARAMAN, A.; BALACHANDRAN, M.; SARAVANAN A. S. **Accounting treatment of goodwill: yesterday, today and tomorrow** Problems and prospects in the international perspective. Journal of Intellectual Capital, vol. 5, n. 1. pp. 131-152. Emerald Group Publishing Limited, 2004.

SETH, A.; SONG, K. P.; PETTIT, R. Value Creation and Destruction in CrossBorder Acquisitions: an Empirical Analysis of Foreign Acquisitions of U.S. Firms. **Strategic Management Journal**, [s. l.], n. 23, p. 921-940, 2002.

SILVA. T. B. J.; LIMA FILHO, R. N.. **Measuring Goodwill: A case study of two companies in the Information Technology sector.** Revista de Estudos Contàbeis, Londrina, v. 5, n. 9, p. 106-126, jul./dez. 2014.

SILVEIRA, F. N. S. **Operationalization of Intangible Asset Measurement Methods in an Electricity Sector Company.** Monograph, 2008. Florianópolis, SC. Federal University of Santa Catarina.

SMITH, M. **Research Methods in Accounting.** London: SAGE, 2003.

STEWART, T. A. **Intellectual Capital.** Rio de Janeiro: Campus, 1998.

WALLIMAN, N. Information, and how to deal with it. **Your Research Project a step-by-step guide for the first-time researcher.** London: SAGE, 2001.

WERNKE, R.; LEMBECK, M.; BORNIA, A. C. **Considerations and comments on intellectual capital.** Revista FAE, v. 6, n. 1, p. 15-26, jan/abr. 2003.

WILSON, R. M. S.; STENSON, J. A. Valuation of information assets on the balance sheet: The recognition and approaches to the valuation of intangible assets. **Business Information Review.** Los Angeles, v. 25, n. 3, p. 167-182, 2008.

ZHANG, D. Intangible Assets and Stock Trading Strategies. **Managerial Finance,** [s.

l.], v. 29, n. 10, 2003.

MIX
Papier aus verantwortungsvollen Quellen
Paper from responsible sources
FSC® C105338

Printed by Books on Demand GmbH, Norderstedt / Germany